Hanging On by a
Thread

Anita Harraway

AuthorHouse™
1663 Liberty Drive
Bloomington, IN 47403
www.authorhouse.com
Phone: 1 (800) 839-8640

Scripture quotations marked NIV are taken from the *Holy Bible, New International Version*®. *NIV*®.
Copyright © 1973, 1978, 1984 by International Bible Society. Used by permission of <u>Zondervan</u>. All rights reserved.

Published by AuthorHouse 02/13/2018

ISBN: 978-1-5246-0050-1 (sc)
978-1-5246-0051-8 (e)

Library of Congress Control Number: 2016912402

Print information available on the last page.

Any people depicted in stock imagery provided by Thinkstock are models,
and such images are being used for illustrative purposes only.
Certain stock imagery © Thinkstock.

This book is printed on acid-free paper.

author**HOUSE**®

CONTENTS

Acknowledgments

I would like to thank God for the power and strength He gave me and my family to overcome tragedy in our lives. He is truly a good and loving God.

Because He lives, I can face tomorrow!

I would like to thank God for blessing me with Quinton, and for the amount time we were given to spend with him; I sure miss him.

I also would like to thank my husband, Virgil, for encouraging me to write this book and for being strong through it all. He was there for me each time I needed him, and I love him more now than ever.

I also want to thank my son Keith for just being my son. I am very proud of him for overcoming a difficult time in his life; Keith is alive today because God spared his life. There are no words I can say to express my appreciation to God for that. I also want to thank Keith for the words of encouragement and the many conversations we had that helped both of us through a very dark time in our lives.

I am grateful and thankful to my parents, siblings, and friends for being there for us through all the anger and frustration. A special thanks to our pastor and church family at that time as well as Cesar Chavez staff and students for all the cards and gifts, prayers, kindness, and support.

Preface

First of all, I want to say that I will never forget the year 2008. It was without a doubt the worst year of my entire life! Two unbearable situations happened that particular year, and my biggest task at that time in my life was surviving each day.

We had a fairly normal life before tragedy hit us like a ton of bricks. I had high hopes for our family, like most people do. My husband had a nice job, we had started a mail-order business, which was a lot of hard work and unfortunately not very lucrative at the time, but I suppose that's how businesses start out.

Our son Keith, who was twenty-three years old at the time, was working and attending college, and our youngest son, Quinton, eighteen years old, was attending high school, eager to graduate in about three months and continue on to the University of Arizona.

My family and I were about to learn the true meaning of "trusting in God."

"For my thoughts are not your thoughts, neither are your ways my ways," declares the Lord.
—Isaiah 55: 8 NIV

I now understand that even though you may feel like you're just hanging on by a thread, God can still heal you and enable you to feel normal again. Yes, it took time, believing, verbalizing my anger, and prayer, but it can be done with the Lord's help.

I want to explain what my version of what hanging on by a thread means.

It means your head feels like it's spinning (not physically but mentally) you don't know what to think about or what not to think about. Your heart aches, aches, and aches! You're afraid of the fear and instability you're feeling and where it might take you. Your bones feel like they hurt, you feel numb, you no longer want to take care of yourself, you want to run away with nowhere to go, and nothing brings you peace—you're simply hanging on by a thread!

That's how I felt in 2008. I was able to hang on because the Lord was able to sustain me with His infinite power.

But he said to me, "My grace is sufficient for you, for my power is made perfect in weakness."
—2 Corinthians 12: 9 NIV

In these pages, I have written about the unbearable situations that happened in 2008, and I've added some heartfelt poems that I wrote to help me transform the frustrations of my wounded heart, which enabled me to conquer the pain of the dreary days to follow.

Quinton, on a sunny afternoon

CHAPTER 1

Quinton's Story

Day 1:

Today was a day like any other day. I was sleeping in late since I had to work the late shift. I was awakened by a phone call; it was a friend of my youngest son. He asked, "Is this Quinton's mom?"

I said yes. A moment later, I was speaking to a paramedic who told me that my son had collapsed. He thought that Quinton had suffered a seizure. The paramedic asked me a few more questions and then told me they were going to transport him to the hospital. I hung up the phone and called my husband and my other son, Keith; Quinton's biological father was also contacted. I got dressed as soon as I could and out the door I went.

Before I go any further, I would like to tell you a little about Quinton. When Quinton was born, I really hadn't settled on a name for him. After I gave birth to him, I remember the hospital giving me a book of names. I looked through it and saw Quinton. The meaning of Quinton is "fifth." (I am sure there are other definitions, but this is the one that was listed.) His brother, Keith, was five years old. I decided that Quinton would be a good name, as he was born five years after his brother. (It seemed logical at the time.) I can honestly say that name suited him well.

At this particular time, Quinton was eighteen years old. It was the end of January 2008, and he was to graduate from high school in May. Quinton was pretty conscientious about his schoolwork, and most of his time, he received good grades. He was on the honor roll quite a few times from elementary to high school. He was naturally smart and enjoyed reading and sports; he played basketball, competed in track, and also played soccer in his younger years. Quinton also enjoyed music, a gift I believe he inherited from his biological father. He learned to play the piano from one of his best friends. We purchased a keyboard for him to sharpen his skills; we listen to a particular song that he programmed in his keyboard sometimes for inspiration and healing. Another important thing I want to mention is that Quinton was a Christian and enjoyed singing in the church choir.

Quinton was pretty ambitious; he liked to keep busy most of the time. Just like any other young person, he had his issues, better known as growing pains. One of the house rules was that before the kids went to school, they were to straighten up their rooms and eat breakfast. Most of the time, he would try to sneak out of the house without doing either. Quinton was thin in stature, and because he was involved in sports, I was very concerned when he would sneak out of the house without breakfast. Of course, he would tell me later he would just buy breakfast at school.

Sometimes Quinton would want something sweet, and he wasn't too cool to get in the kitchen and bake something. He made oatmeal cake a few times. (All I can say is the cake was thick, and it did taste like oatmeal.)

Even though his room was never clean (well, not up to my standards), somehow he seemed to get away with it by sneaking out of the house so he could get to school a little earlier than expected.

Quinton really enjoyed Christmas, just as I do; it was one of his favorite holidays. I loved to see him get excited when that time of year came around. Even as the boys got older, we all tried to pick out a tree together. We tried to keep the traditions alive. When we would go Christmas shopping together, Quinton would watch and see what items in the store I would say I really liked. That's how he would figure out what he was going to get me. (Pretty smart, huh?)

A few weeks before Quinton collapsed, we were sitting at the computer, getting him ready for college. We were trying to figure out what section of the campus his dorms were in. That was an exciting time for both of us; he was really excited about attending college.

On the day he collapsed at school, Quinton was running track. Unfortunately, the worst thing possible happened: my son had suffered a massive heart attack. I drove to the hospital as fast as I could. When I arrived at the Banner Good Samaritan Hospital, my family and I were in a private waiting room, and the doctors were informing us the best they could. It was all so overwhelming!

I eventually left the room and stood on the corner of the hallway outside the waiting room just to get some air. As I stood there, numb, I noticed a hospital employee standing to the right of me, not too far away. The employee eventually came up to me and gave me a neatly folded blue sheet. I don't remember him saying anything besides, "Here you go." I held on to that blue sheet the entire time I was there at the hospital. Somehow it gave me a little bit of comfort.

After Quinton was transported to the hospital, he had two operations back to back. Our family was finally able to see him four or five hours later; he looked like a different person. His whole body was all puffed up and swollen. The doctors told us if he made it through the night, they would be able to transfer him to the Mayo Clinic. They also said he would be eligible for a heart transplant. All I remember is being in shock that night at the hospital. I cried and cried and prayed our son would not be taken from us. It was almost like I felt the pain my son was going through. I have never felt pain like that before. I am very thankful for the support of family and friends and all the prayers.

Day 2:

Thank God, Quinton survived through the night and was stable enough to be moved to a different hospital the next day. Some of my family members arrived at the hospital to show much-needed support. Today we learned that Quinton suffered from a congenital heart disorder. The clinical term is *congenital coronary artery anomalies.*

Day 3:

Quinton continues his fight, and we continue to pray. Incisions were made in both legs to remove pressure. Another procedure was done to remove blood clots from around the heart. After the procedures were done, Keith, Quinton's brother, brought Quinton's iPod to make sure Quinton could listen to some of his favorite tunes. We all continue to talk to him and also rub his hands and forehead.

Day 4:

As each day goes by, we all continue to trust God for a miracle. I purchased a journal in order to record all that Quinton was going through. (The journal was for Quinton to keep and read once he was able to.)

At that time, I had been a Christian for over twelve years and had seen and heard many testimonies regarding the healing power of God. I and other family members believed for his full recovery. I remember how much I trusted God to heal Quinton and bring him through this very difficult time. My faith was strong, even when the doctors would come in and tell us things we didn't want to hear. I am so grateful for the strength that God gave me and my family through this difficult time. Even though my faith was strong, my mind warred against me (which is normal, especially when Quinton was faced with a new challenge in his body).

Our son was in for the fight of his life, and as his mother, if I didn't believe with my whole heart for God to heal him, I would have failed him. I don't remember which day we finally went home for the night to rest in our bed, but when my husband and I finally went home, I wrote down some Scriptures and affirmations to focus on and to keep our faith strong:

Trust in the Lord with all your heart and lean not on your own understanding; in all your ways acknowledge him, and he will make your paths straight.

—Proverbs 3:5 NIV

With long life will I satisfy him and show him my salvation.

—Psalm 91:16 NIV

I lift up my eyes to the hills—where does my help come from? My help comes from the Lord, the maker of heaven and Earth. He will not let your foot slip; he who watches over you will not slumber; indeed, he who watches over Israel will neither slumber nor sleep. The Lord watches over you; the Lord is your shade at your right hand; the sun will not harm you by day, nor the moon by night. The Lord will keep you from all harm; he will watch over your life; the Lord will watch over your coming and going, both now and forevermore.—Psalm 121:1–8 NIV

The Lord is my light and my salvation—whom shall I fear? The Lord is the stronghold of my life—of whom shall I be afraid? When evil men advance against me to devour my flesh, when my enemies and my foe attack me, they will stumble and fall. Though an army besiege me, my heart will not fear; though war break out against me, even then will I be confident. One thing I ask of the Lord, this is what I seek: that I may dwell in the house of the Lord all the days of my life, to gaze upon the beauty of the Lord and to seek him in his temple. For in the day of trouble he will keep me safe in his dwelling; he will hide me in the shelter of his tabernacle and set me high upon a rock.

Then my head will be exalted above the enemies who surround me; at his tabernacle will I sacrifice with shouts of joy; I will sing and make music to the Lord. Hear my voice when I call, O Lord; be merciful to me and answer me. My heart says of you, Seek his face! Your face, Lord, I will seek. Do not hide your face from me, do not turn your servant away in anger; you have been my helper. Do not reject me or forsake me, O God my Savior. Though my father and mother forsake me, the Lord will receive me.

Teach me your way, O Lord; lead me in a straight path because of my oppressors. Do not turn me over to the desire of my foes, for false witnesses rise up against me, breathing out violence. I am still confident of this: I will see the goodness of the Lord in the land of the living. Wait for the Lord; be strong and take heart and wait for the Lord.—Psalms 27:1–14 NIV

I will not die but live, and will proclaim what the Lord has done.

—Psalms 118:17 NIV

"No weapon forged against you will prevail, and you will refute every tongue that accuses you. This is the heritage of the servants of the Lord, and this is their vindication from me," declares the Lord.

—Isaiah 54:17 NIV

But he was pierced for our transgressions, he was crushed for our iniquities; the punishment that brought us peace was upon him, and by his wounds we are healed.

—Isaiah 53:5 NIV

So do not fear, for I am with you; do not be dismayed, for I am your God. I will strengthen you and help you; I will uphold you with my righteous right hand.

—Isaiah 41:10 NIV

Believing God

I remember while at the hospital, (at this point, we had been at the hospital about four days) I visualized myself kneeling before God in heaven, and even though my son Quinton was pretty tall, I visualized myself holding him in my arms like a small child. I was holding him up to the Lord and saying, "Your will be done." That was one of the hardest things I had to do. I know now that when someone leaves us, it could be his or her time to leave this earth or maybe they're just ready to go. (Nobody knows)

The Bible says, "God's ways are not our ways." He knows the beginning from the end! He knows all. Even though I gave the situation over to God, I still said to God, "Just please don't decide to take my son from me. I will do anything you say, just don't take my son from me." But in my heart, I knew God knew best and God already knew how this terrible situation was going to turn out. This was a tug-of-war on my heart!

Day 5:

I was feeling so much anguish; I asked God, "What else can I do besides pray?" and He impressed upon both my husband and I that we should go on a fast. We did not fast from eating food; we were too weak to do that. Our fast consisted of vegetables and liquids.

Today, the doctor mentioned Quinton's heart was working better. We were extremely happy for this good news. The nurse was also using a nerve stimulator on Quinton today. The neurologist let us know that Quinton's brain had some swelling. Quinton's biological father was sitting with him and told me and my husband that while he was holding Quinton's hand, Quinton moved his hand a little bit and also opened his eyes. Amazing!

Day 6:

While visiting Quinton today, we witnessed his eyes opening and him responding to noise. He also responded when his hands were held. On one occasion, Virgil witnessed Quinton's eyes open all the way. I didn't see it at the time; I must have been looking down. We were very happy, and when I finally looked at Quinton after Virgil mentioned his eyes were open, he was looking directly at me and blinked. Hope welled up inside of me! This was a very exciting day for us. It seemed Quinton was making progress, and that was encouraging.

My husband and I purchased a plant for Quinton to place in his room for him to see once he was released from the hospital. For me, the plant represented life. I believed Quinton would fully recover.

Day 7:

We continued to read and play music for Quinton. As I was talking to Quinton, I asked him if he could hear me, and if so to open his eyes for me. His body started twitching, and he eventually opened his eyes.

Today the nurse mentioned to us that Quinton had coughed before we came in to visit him. During that same visit, Quinton looked like he was coughing, and I asked the nurse what was happening. She said he was coughing, and that coughing was a good thing. Friends and family continued to show support and pray for Quinton's full recovery. My sister was there that day to visit Quinton. She mentioned how she stood at the foot of his bed, and Quinton opened his eyes and looked directly at her. She was amazed that this happened, and I was very happy to hear it too. When a loved one is hanging on to life, any movement is a sign of hope.

Day 8:

I remember on this particular day, Quinton was really looking good. Quinton's right hand moved, and he picked it up. It almost seemed as if he was trying to talk.

The internal medicine doctor said they are going to start Quinton on liquid food because his stomach was working; wow, that was good news. I felt our prayers were getting through and that we were seeing slow progress. All progress is a miracle to us. Both my husband and I had a dream of Quinton today, which I will explain later.

Day 9:

We continue to believe for progress.

Day 10: February 9, 2008

Quinton really looked good this day. He had been dealing with tremors frequently, and this day he seemed to have settled down a little. My husband and I were visiting during the evening hours. It was a little before eight o'clock, and we said our good-byes to Quinton for a little while; we were going to go downstairs and get some dinner. We were gone from his room around forty minutes or so, and when we finished dinner we went to sit in the hospital lobby. As we were sitting there, a doctor swiftly approached us and said, "Your son is leaving us—you need to come now!"

We got up and took that indescribable, awful trip up the elevator to be with Quinton. Quinton was gone before we got there. Shock and disbelief started to set in at that point. I felt numb! This may sound strange, but I don't remember crying at all when we entered Quinton's room and I saw him lying there, gone!

Shortly after his passing, the doctor told us that the neurologist would have to do a brain scan to make sure there was no more brain activity. My husband and I were present and also Quinton's biological father. The brain scan was done on him, and there was no brain activity—a confirmation that he was really gone.

I believed with everything within me that my son would live. I was lost, in shock, and numb. I remember yelling about something the neurologist said about his temperature—I don't remember the details, but I started to feel those erratic emotions rising inside of me. My husband and I didn't stay in the room very long with Quinton, but we returned to the quiet, enclosed waiting room where we were sleeping in at the hospital. I don't remembering crying at this point, just feeling numb and lifeless.

My husband and I went back to Quinton's room a while later. I'm not sure how much time had passed. As we walked down that hallway to Quinton's room, it was a slow, dreary walk to see Quinton. The walk seemed a lot longer than it was. We reached Quinton's room, and I remembered being upset with him since I had told him daily to keep hanging on. The pain hit me all at once, and I was completely doubled over in pain and grief; our son was gone, and there was nothing I could do. I didn't have a choice but to say good-bye.

When we returned home, I remember standing next to my bed and saying to the Lord, "You are a healer, and I really need you to heal me." I had faith He would heal me even though I did not know how He was going to take away *the worst pain I had ever felt in my life!*

I have been a Christian for a while, and I knew God would be faithful and heal me and my family. Again, I will say I didn't know *how* God was going to heal me, but I knew He would be faithful to me once again. I also wanted confirmation that my son was really in heaven. Even though I already had one confirmation, I needed to know for sure. So I asked God for another confirmation that Quinton was really in heaven.

The Comfort of a Blanket

To the hospital I raced to be by my son's side;
His life was coming to an end you see, from this reality I could not hide.

As family members stood in a small room, I, outside that room, standing on a corner of
the wall,
A man walked up to me and handed me a blue sheet, just a blue sheet, that's all.

Praying to God to spare my boy's life as I held on to the soft sheet, the day completely tragic;
I knew by holding that sheet it was God's peace, God's peace in the form of fabric.

I held the neatly folded blue sheet while staring at the floor, with just fabric to cling;
The soft blue sheet I held was giving me warmth and comfort that only a blanket can bring.

❖ I still have that blue sheet. It's tucked away in my dresser drawer.

CHAPTER 2

The Three Dreams

First dream:

My son, Keith, had the first dream while Quinton was in the hospital. He came to my husband and me and said that he had a dream that Quinton would regain consciousness with a cough. As I wrote previously, on day seven, the nurse in the hospital mentioned to us that Quinton had indeed coughed a few times. We believed at that time this was a sign that he was really conscious and he could hear us then and the previous days; and we believed that he was on his way to a complete recovery.

Second dream:

I had the second dream two days before Quinton passed away. I dreamed that I saw Quinton lying in a regular hospital bed without any tubes in him; the only thing in the room was him lying in the bed. He raised his left arm and waved it as if he was beckoning me to come. He looked completely normal. The previous day, before the dream, I had been trying to get Quinton to move his arm.

My interpretation of this dream is the arm that Quinton was moving in the dream was a symbol that Quinton could now move his arm, and he was in his perfect heavenly body. I didn't realize that at the time of the dream, but I did later on after he passed away.

Third dream:

My husband had the third dream. We both had a dream about Quinton the same night. I told my husband about the dream I had about Quinton, and he said that he had a dream as well. He had a dream that he saw

Quinton in heaven standing between both of us, and Quinton had a smile on his face and had a gold heart. As he was telling me about the dream, I got a little angry; I was thinking, *does this mean Quinton is going to die?*

Another thing happened as my husband was telling me about his dream; I was able to visualize everything he was saying as he was telling me the dream. But I saw some things a little different. I saw Quinton in heaven, standing between me and my husband. Quinton had on a white robe and the middle section of Quinton's body was translucent so I could see his golden heart. Quinton had a big smile on his face and was doing a fancy little dance. Later on, I called my mom because I didn't know what to make of this dream, and it made me very upset.

The Golden Heart

After I mentioned to my mom about the third dream, she told my sister about the dream, and my sister remembered she saw a figurine in a store of a boy with a golden heart. They both went to the store to purchase the figurine for me before the funeral. After the funeral, our family members were leaving our house, and my mom gave me a box, I opened it, pulled out a figurine of a boy holding a golden heart, and stared at the figurine in awe! It was one of the most beautiful things I had ever seen; it was as if God was speaking directly to me when I picked up the figurine. I felt like that figurine was made just for me and that God had answered my prayer.

I felt like God was letting me know that my son was indeed in heaven! I cherish that figurine; it is one of my favorite possessions. God truly does answer prayers.

Lost

How do I find my way when the path has disappeared but the darkness, anger, and agony are consuming and so very clear?

Wondering if I will stay lucid or even continue to breathe; somehow with the hope inside me, I am still able to perceive. I must believe in the One I know who truly cares as I step onto a path that is neither here nor there.

There is great pain as I ly inside of torture and misery; I know He can cut through the layers of pain, if only I continue to believe. His deliverance will come in time to me, but His method is not something that I can figure out or be able to see.

As I continue to stagger, wondering if my steps will ever be firm and complete, in time I know He'll faithfully create a new path under my adrift, weary feet.

CHAPTER 3

The Grief Process

The process of grieving for a child is hard to put into words. If I could describe it, it would be as if a woman were giving birth in reverse. When a woman gives birth, she has great labor pains and anguish trying to push the baby out into the world. Losing a child feels like you're having the pains of childbirth, but while doubled over in pain and anguish, you're watching your child leave this world instead of enter it.

Losing a child also feels horrifying. I felt like I was screaming inside at times without being able to verbalize it. It feels like you are going to jump out of your skin. And that hopeless feeling of not being able to stop your child from dying is indescribable. I felt like at times I was losing my mind and wanted to run away. I felt weak and extremely vulnerable. I didn't know if I would ever be happy again; I felt like at times I didn't know what extreme I was going to go to in order to ease the pain. That feeling scared me because I felt like I was losing myself. I felt like I was experiencing physical pains in my stomach. As weak as I was, I knew God was with me. He promises never to leave us or forsake us.

At this point, our family has a long road ahead of us. One month after burying Quinton, our other son, Keith, went through a very serious ordeal. I won't tell all the details, but the unthinkable happened. My son's car was shot at several times while he was driving, and when he raised his hand to his face to protect himself from the bullets a bullet lodged in his hand. God protected him and spared his life!

My husband and I are so grateful to the Lord for the unbelievable miracle of sparing our son's life. This added another extreme situation to all of our lives while we were in the process of grieving for Quinton. All this turmoil felt like a thunderstorm in my head.

We were suddenly involved in a legal battle. When dealing with the legal system there are a lot of ups and downs. Throughout the process, my husband and I could feel the Lord's strength. It was so much for all of us to handle. It was a day to day struggle for all of us.

We didn't have the money we needed to pay the attorney, but a few family members gracefully help us out. We didn't know where the money was going to come from, but the Lord provided for us. We are grateful for their help and kindness and will never forget it! A few months went by, and I eventually went back to my part-time night job to help out financially.

Back to Work and Losing Hope

I decided to go back to work. My husband and I had a small business, and I also had a part-time job I worked in the evenings. I figured going back to work would not only help financially but emotionally. As they say, keeping busy helps keep your mind off of your problems.

I worked for a few months and was having a lot of trouble. I wasn't really able to focus on my job and didn't know what to do since I really needed to work. I considered going to a support group, but I never did. I am sure it would have helped me tremendously. I am thankful for family members who were there for me whenever I needed to talk and couldn't keep it together; they listened gracefully and tried to console me as much as possible.

My mind wandered a lot at work, and I had many outbursts of tears; I would try to find places at work to cry in private when those outbursts happened. There were staff members that took the time to talk with me, and I felt so grateful for their caring support. I will never forget it. I felt like I was starting to have problems physically, but wasn't sure what was going on with me. I would see dark spots. I would take a step, and it seemed like the ground was not under my feet. I had pains in my stomach, and I felt in a way that I was slowly dying inside.

I remember wanting to run away from it all. There was no way I could have done this since my husband and I were in the middle of the legal battle involving our son; how cruel of me to think that way.

I remember thinking about where I could go to escape all of the pain. But each time I started to think of running away, I would remember my husband and my son Keith. They needed me, and how would I feel if either one of them ran away from me? I finally realized that staying with my family and facing the pain was the only thing I could do. After all, we were all going through this together.

One day at work, it was busy and I was not feeling very well. There were children running around almost knocking over racks of clothes, and I remember looking at them and not having the strength to tell them to stop. I was standing there getting ready to take a step, and I felt my nervous system was shutting down (that is the best way I can describe how I felt). I just knew something terrible was going on with me physically, and I knew I had gone back to work too soon. I eventually left my job even though we really needed the money.

At this time, I was thinking of my son Quinton's graduation. Quinton passed away in February, a few months before he was to graduate from high school. I wore Quinton's cap and gown for him, and my husband and I were honored to accept Quinton's diploma for him.

Before the graduation, I did not know how I was going to handle it emotionally, and I remembered praying to God for strength for the both of us. During the graduation, I felt numb, and I now know that was the Lord helping me get through the ceremony. He helped me by not allowing me to feel a lot of emotion. I am thankful for that. Again, a person never knows when he or she prays to God for help just how He is going to help. In this case, as I mentioned, I just felt numb to the emotions of the graduation.

Quinton's graduation 2008

Quinton's high school graduation

I slept a lot in the months following the graduation. I didn't do much of anything, only the basics. I was in survival mode at that time. So was my husband, who had done an excellent job of keeping things together. I have always known he was a stable, strong man, but he really proved himself through this extremely tough time in all of our lives. We were, after all, dealing with Quinton's death, and then Keith was almost killed and was now in jail, we had legal fees to pay, and we had to close our business. I no longer wanted the business, nor were we able to keep it. I remember not caring about too much of anything at that time. And I was not working, which did not help the situation. What a terrible time!

Months later, I needed to finish taking care of closing our mail-order business. I remember lying in the bed one day looking at the floor in my bedroom that was covered in paperwork that I needed to tend to. I was still very weak emotionally and physically at this time; I remember my husband having to help out a lot with the housework and meals at that time because I just didn't have the strength. I remember looking at those papers in the floor and saying to myself, "I really need to finish closing the business out." And one day, before I knew it, I was out of that bed sorting through and filing those papers.

That was just one of the times I felt God giving me strength to do something I absolutely had no physical or mental strength to do on my own. God says in His Word, "His strength is made perfect in our weakness."

The Vision of My Son (September 2008)

I cried out to the Lord in pain many nights asking Him to turn back time. That may sound funny or ridiculous to you, but I was very serious. I knew God could do anything, and I was asking Him for that. I was praying and asking the Lord to see my son again. You know, I wanted to be able to have a vision of him in heaven. After all, there are other people that have written books about such things, why would I be any different?

Then it happened—I had a vision of my son! In the vision, I was standing in the doorway of Quinton's old bedroom. I saw Quinton, but he seemed a little shorter. His eyes looked funny as if he were older. He seemed to have gray hair. I finally realized what I was seeing was light reflecting from his hair and eyes.

He handed me a book and said, "I'm giving my book back to you."

I said, "No, it's your book."

We went back and forth for a while until I finally accepted the book from him. When Quinton said, "I came to give my book back to you."

At the time of the vision, I did not know what book he was referring to.

In the next part of the vision, we were sitting side by side. Quinton was sitting a little lower than me, our heads leaning together, and I had one arm wrapped around his shoulders. The hug was very warming to my heart; I could feel some of the brokenness in my heart being healed. Quinton didn't say anything else at this point. I got up and walked out of the room, and when I re-entered the room Quinton was gone. There was a bed with a blue sheet and a pillow that was wrinkled as if someone had been sitting there.

The blue sheet was the exact same color of the sheet that the hospital employee gave me when I first arrived at the hospital. That comforting blue sheet!

The following morning after the vision, I was so excited and told my husband about it. I said to him, "I don't know what book Quinton gave to me." My husband thought about it for a few minutes, and he reached into his nightstand and pulled out a book—it was the journal I was keeping for Quinton while we were in the hospital believing for his recovery. That was the book Quinton gave back to me. The final fulfillment of the vision came the next morning.

Recorded in the journal were Scriptures and positive affirmations. The next morning as I was waking up, there was a Scripture that was swimming around in my mind and on my lips; it was as if I were saying the words as I was waking up. The words to the Scripture are, "So is my word that goes out from my mouth: It will not return to me empty, but will accomplish what I desire and achieve the purpose for which I sent it" (Isa. 55:11). NIV

God's Word is a living and active, and His Word will accomplish what it says it will accomplish, just maybe not in the way we envision.

As Quinton returned the journal to me, it was as if God was saying He had fulfilled all the Scriptures I had believed on in His way. During the beginning stages of my grieving process, I kept saying and thinking that I was not going to make it, and the Lord was allowing Quinton to give those very same Scriptures I had written for him back to me to aid me in my healing process.

Clarity about the Dream

- When I asked the Lord to be able to see my son, it wasn't because I wanted guidance or to ask why? I simply wanted to have a vision of my son.

- I do believe I saw my son as he is in heaven (an image of him) because of the light that was shining on him and also because that's what I asked God for. I don't have any recollection of what his body looked like in this vision.

- I believe when we have dreams or visions of loved ones, God is using an *image* of the person in order to show us guidance; it's not the deceased loved one guiding us, it's God.

I Am Still Grateful

I am extremely grateful for all of the love and support from family and friends. We appreciate all of the kindness and thoughtfulness from everyone.

I thank God every time I see my oldest son Keith; he was in jail for about a year after the ordeal, but he's out now and doing just fine. He believes in God, and many things have turned around for him because he didn't give up! Things were extremely tough on him for a number of years, and it was a struggle for me and my husband to watch him go through it. I know he has learned much about life in a very short amount of time. Some life lessons can be painfully hard and difficult, but life lessons become valuable for us once that particular lesson is over. Keith is a smart, resourceful, and caring person, and my husband and I are very proud of him.

I have learned the true meaning of humility during this difficult process. I said to my husband one day, "Is God going to help me if I'm angry at Him?"

"Of course He will help you; He understands," my husband said.

I felt like we didn't deserve any of this. To me, it just wasn't right. I realize now that other people do not understand the kind of pain you are feeling when you lose someone close to you (unless they have experienced it themselves). I remember getting angry at other people for trying to give me a Scripture to ease my pain or say things that are completely insensitive to our situation. I know now that when you lose someone, other people are only trying to help in their own way, even though it felt annoying to me at times.

Some people try to help you by checking in on you to make sure that you are okay. Other friends or family members say nothing while some pat you on the back and say it'll be okay. Others quote the Bible to you, hoping you will just get over it because a Scripture from the Bible is being quoted.

And let me add, I'm sure at some point in my life I have said something insensitive to someone who has lost a loved one or someone going through a difficult time without even realizing it. When a person loses someone, other people are not going to say and do just the right thing at the right time; I know that now, I'm simply expressing the frustrations I felt. When a person loses a loved one, that person needs space and support; it's impossible for others to know what that person needs at just the right time.

Even though Quinton passed away, we are so grateful that we were able to spend nine days with him after the initial day he collapsed to say good-bye. Even though we didn't know we were saying good-bye at the time, we were still given that precious time with him, and for that, we are eternally grateful.

Quinton lived nine days following his accident. My family's world changed in 2008. I am not even the same person; I feel more humble and grateful for each day. I can now see the beauty and the uniqueness in people that I never saw before. I have learned a very important fact through our challenges, and that is there are some things that a person has no control over. When you can't do anything about a situation, you have to give that situation over to God to handle. A priority in my life is staying focused on the good in life since there's so much negativity all around us.

I now know that when we put our trust in God we must know that He is all-knowing, and He will make the best decision for us. God knows the beginning to the end and everything in between. I didn't have a choice except to believe God's decision was the best one.

I have some of Quinton's belongings in every room of our house, and I have continued to leave the light on in his room at night since the day we lost him. Somehow this helps me. I still have the precious gift of memories, (this was one of my poems) and when each memory of Quinton occurs, it is now truly a gift and not torture.

I gave birth to him and then lost him, but because Quinton was a Christian, he's alive in heaven forever. I'm grateful my son is in heaven and that we will see him again someday. Through all of the pain and agony and the many days I felt lost and all the sleepless nights, I can still say, "I trust the Lord with all my heart." I trust God because He has given me the strength to laugh again and not feel guilty about it.

God has also given me the grace to no longer feel obligated to hold on to the pain of losing my son for fear of dishonoring him. Hanging on by a thread no longer means that I'm consumed by tragedy, but how God's strength and grace allowed me to make it through that tragedy. I sure miss my son.

Even though I had to say good-bye to him, I know he's just fine.

God's Decision

What will be the end result°… when my life was abruptly altered, and I cried out to Him? I need help and strength as the light of my son's life seems to quickly grow dim.

What will be the end result°… while my son is hanging on to his precious life as I told him to do; was he listening to me or walking toward the light to start anew?

What will be the end result°… while believing with my whole heart with enough faith to create a change; yes, my faith was sufficient, but was I believing something that would never be regained?

What will be the end result°… is there something, anything I can do more? I would give my life to be able to kick open that completely sealed door.

The end result was heaven, with open arms he was received; happy and tortured is my heart, you see, it is God's final decision I must struggle to believe.

Thunderstorm

It came in the middle of the night; there was not a single warning.
The loud burst of thunder and the rapid pace of rain would not let up till the shine of the
morning came.

Looking out at the storm, it felt so violent and reckless,
ready to consume my house, the trees, and the earth
in just a matter of seconds.

My house continues to shift and sway,
wishing for the sunlight to peek through—looking for the break of day.

After the storm has released its anger and broken branches all around,
I walked through the puddles and mud greeting the warm smile of the sun.
I reached down and picked the branches up, one by one.

Dedicated to my favorite oldest son, Keith

Who Will Listen?

Who will listen as time passes by;
My heart still tender, my eyes I still dry.

Life goes on is the attitude I must take,
But sorrow is there to flood my heart to break.

As I whimper, they don't hear the sound of thunder in my soul;
They only hear the whistling of a wind that continually blows.

Who will listen when I cry and sadness finds me today?
If they can't hear me cry, I'm sure they won't know what to say.

My heart breaks when I can't talk about the pain;
I suppose no words can fill the void of emptiness; no words to explain.

Why don't they think about, why don't they talk about the shadows of agony that still remain? The wounds are hidden deep but exposed just the same.

I wish I had the power to turn back the hand of time, or maybe if only there was a way I could have stopped that unthinkable crime.

Looking back on the cloud of darkness that seemed to flood my entire space, the darkness is still visible at times, in the mirror, on my face.

No person can fix or heal the pain that has wrongfully occurred°… Humbled I have become, with my face to the ground, knowing He won't let my tears of thunder go unheard.

Dedicated to my favorite youngest son Quinton

CHAPTER 4

Just a Little Bit More about Quinton

Quinton received several awards throughout his school years, including Student of the Month, advanced reader awards, Math and spelling awards, and five honors roll awards.

Quinton was accepted into a few colleges, but he chose University of Arizona, where he wanted to study engineering.

Another one of Quinton's accomplishments was he had the opportunity to go on a twenty-mile hike through the Grand Canyon with one of his uncles. That hike was challenging for him because once the hike was complete, his uncle informed him that they needed to walk two more miles to get to the hotel! (No ride to pick them up.) Needless to say, Quinton was not happy with his uncle! I was very impressed by Quinton's courage to even agree to go on that hike! (His poor legs must have been so tired.)

There was a small gesture that Quinton made that I'll never forget. I am a coffee drinker, and the day before Mother's Day (I believe Quinton was fourteen at the time) Quinton asked me, "Can you show me how to make coffee so I can make it for you in the morning?" For some reason that kind gesture really made me feel special. It's not the big things we do for others that make the most impact in their lives.

I would say Quinton lived a very fulfilling life. He was a Christian, he had family and friends that loved him very much, and he loved music, sports, and aspired to be the best student he could! One thing I used to tell him when he was still with us was, "You're my favorite youngest son." I loved Quinton for just being my son; he didn't even mind hanging out with me, at least when he wasn't mad at me. I still have all the greeting cards he's given me, and I read them from time to time. I miss his smile and his sense of humor, but I will always have the gift of a memory!

Quinton's selfie

A day at Disneyland

Keith and Quinton

Quinton waking up from a nap

There's Only One

The question I was asked is, "How many do you have?" I said, "Only one."
To say more would say too much;
It's best to keep my answer simple, not wordy, but blunt.

How many do you have? I said, "Only one."
If I tell you much more, it will be too complex,
Time-consuming, and tears may follow next.

How many do you have? I said, "Only one."
I no longer see one anymore; he's safe in God's care.
I had to make peace with having only one; it took time, perseverance, and a lot of prayer.

How many do you have? I said, "Only one."
I don't talk about this much, but sometimes I do.
I have only one with me, but God blessed me with two.

When I See You

There are memories that are engraved in my mind—
Your personality, your smile, and the times we just hung out for a little while.

The memories never go away, but are always there;
I will always have them to ponder—and always to share.

The memories are left here in place of you;
They satisfy my emotions and feelings and of course when I'm missing you.

When I see you in other young men that cross my path—warmth and sadness always wash over me.
A reminder, a glimpse, of how you used to be.

When my memories someday collide with eternity,
That's when I will see you.

We will all be together again to experience your personality, your smile, and we'll be able to hang out for a long, long while.

A New Beginning

My days are no longer tumultuous as the years gone by.
Being able to laugh and smile is a benefit of trusting God, time passing, and releasing my cries.

I can't go back and change the dreadful days, months, and years,
But I do see a new day, the echo of a new sound I can clearly hear.

I know that sound; it carries a pitch in which my wounded soul has been depleted.
I hear that glorious new sound walking forward, feeling normal; I'm so happy I can finally hear it.

Quinton's Grand Canyon hike

Quinton at the Grand Canyon

The end of my journey

"The Father" I Married

You were the one who was meant to be there, even from the very beginning.
How do you let them know you care and that you're here for their protection?
Even though you were determined and committed you'd still have to face their rejection?

As you concentrated on staying focused and being the best father that you could, you did see glimpses of appreciation, realizing you were starting to be understood.

When things got rough, you didn't cower and hide; you stayed and dug in your heels, your determination and prayers were not denied.

Now the respect is there, the tug of war is finally ending.
You didn't need to wait for them to consider you as their father because that's who you are, that's who you've been, from the very beginning.

Even though your name is not on their birth certificates, and you were not in the room when they were born, unbeknownst to you, their lives were yours to carry.
You found them and they found you, and you became their father; and that's the father that I married.

Dedicated to my husband, Virgil, on Father's Day 2015

The Gift of a Memory

A fond memory, it just happens, a thought I didn't plan.
The peace and comfort it brings is like a smile washing over my soul released from God's hand.

The memories I have make you feel so very near; of course, this must be
Your disciplined and giving spirit are simply active inside of me.

When a memory occurs, I can clearly see
That—that very memory was created right on time, just for me.

A memory comes to me when I expect it the least; it seems to be a gift for that moment of mine,
Filling in that void that will close someday, in time.

Your memory is like a breath of fresh air to my stormy, unsettled heart;
These memories are like having you here with me, even though for now we're apart.

Dedicated to my husband, Virgil, in memory of his mom, Mary Harraway
May 2014

Epilogue

Today, December 15th 2015, it's been almost eight years since Quinton's passing.

During this time, I've learned a lot about grief and how it can affect your life. I've learned that the way people grieve over the death of a loved one varies from one person to another, and there's no right or wrong way to do it.

I know that this kind of grief can make you feel completely lost, and the pain one feels is overwhelmingly torturous. I don't have a formula for how to endure this kind of pain, but there are some things that I did that helped me.

After my son died, I prayed to God for healing so that I could function and not walk around sad and depressed the rest of my life.

He heals the brokenhearted and binds up their wounds.

—Psalms 147:3 NIV

My family was there for me in that they allowed me to vent my frustrations and anger by just listening and at times giving me advice. I read a few books on grief given to me by family members that also helped me when I was strong enough to read them.

Inside, I felt so terrible that I wanted to do something completely drastic to fix the pain, like run away; but I couldn't. From what I'm told, that pain will follow you wherever you are, so facing it where you are is best.

There is one more thing I want to mention. I believed I would somehow make it through this crisis way down deep inside me. Even though I didn't feel like it was ever going to happen, I believed that God would bring me through, and you know what, He did! I no longer feel angry, depressed, or lost. He gave me the strength to walk through that overwhelmingly tortuous pain.

He gives strength to the weary and increases the power of the weak.

—Isaiah 40: 29 NIV

About the Author

Anita Harraway shares her painful journey of how she endured almost losing two children in one year.

She is currently a homemaker who loves to help people in practical ways and enjoys writing poetry. She has been happily married for almost twenty years and views God and family as top priorities in her life. Anita and her family currently reside in the sunny state of Arizona.

Amazon.com,

BarnesandNoble.com

ajhbooks@centurylink.net